GET YOUR MONEY RIGHT

IT'S LEVELS TO THIS

LEVEL ZERO:
LAYING THE FOUNDATION

Mind Over Money, LLC

MIND OVER MONEY

IT'S LEVELS TO THIS

LEVEL ZERO:
LAYING THE FOUNDATION

The workbook to uncover personal financial
biases and set a mindset for building wealth

Level Zero:Laying the Foundation

This level is all about creating a space of belief and doing some introspection. You need to believe in why the journey you're about to take is worth it. It's about understanding why you have certain reservations and habits with money. It's about uncovering past experiences that may deter you from truly seeking your financial freedom.

This level is about building the grit to push through and keep chasing your goals even when it gets hard because it will get hard. You will want to quit when you have your first setback. You will get frustrated when you make the same mistake that you've already made seven times. You will have doubt that you can ever change.

MIND OVER MONEY

Its Levels To This

But you have to keep going.
You have to learn to forgive yourself when you make mistakes. You have to believe that what you're doing is worth it and that you can do this.

Because you can.

Here we are, laying the foundation. **It matters**. **It matters a lot**. When you are solid on the on the ins and outs of why you're doing what you're doing, it makes the hard stuff easier to go up against.

So get ready, you'll be answering some tough questions. If you're honest with yourself, you'll learn a little more about why you do some of the things you do and how you can change those things to get on a path to becoming better with your finances.

First, let's talk about who you are. There are many things that can shape us. You will focus on the impact that money has on who you are. This will help you discover financial biases you may have and address attitudes toward money

MIND OVER MONEY

Who are you?

  Name: _____

  Age: _____

  Key Characteristics (Describe yourself to someone meeting you for the first time. i.e profession, lifestyle, demeanor, etc.)

_____

_____

_____

_____

_____

Who are you when you "have money"?

  Describe how you interact with others, how you treat yourself, thoughts you have, etc.

_____

_____

_____

_____

_____

MIND OVER MONEY

ITS LEVELS TO THIS

Who

Who are you when you don't "have money"?
Describe how you interact with others, how you
treat yourself, thoughts you have, etc.

Who do you want to be?

MIND OVER MONEY

Its Levels to This

Who

Who helped shape how you handle your finances?

Who do you trust talking to about money issues?

Who would you take advice from? Are these the same person? Why or why not?

M MIND OVER MONEY

ITS LEVELS TO THIS

Next, let's talk about what you are doing and feeling. Sometimes we ignore behaviors that we know are detrimental to our goals because we don't want to address the core of the actual problem. Now is the time to work through that and think forward.

What scares you about conquering your finances?

_____

_____

_____

_____

_____

What are your top three goals?
- ☐ Save for major purchase
- ☐ Get out of credit card debt
- ☐ Pay off student loans
- ☐ Save for vacation
- ☐ Save for retirement
- ☐ Increase Giving
- ☐ Build Emergency Fund
- ☐ Other:_____

MIND over MONEY

Its Levels to This

What

What actions prevented you from reaching your goals in the past?

What are two actions you can implement now to work on reaching your goals?

MIND OVER MONEY

ITS LEVELS TO THIS

What

What does your ideal financial situation look like in one year?

_____

_____

_____

five years?

_____

_____

_____

ten years?

_____

_____

_____

twenty years?

_____

_____

_____

The next aspect we will tackle is where your physical location is, where you money goes and how all of these things came to be. It is important to realize that the playing field is not level. You may have started with a disadvantage. Acknowledge that.

Where

Where do you live?

- ☐ Live w/ parents or relative (rent free)
- ☐ Renting w/roommate
- ☐ Renting alone
- ☐ Own home
- ☐ Other: _____

Are you content with your current housing situation?   Yes   No

Does where you live impact your ability to reach your financial goals? If so, how?

_____

_____

_____

_____

_____

_____

Where

Where does most of your money go?
- ☐ Debt payments
- ☐ Rent/ Mortgage
- ☐ Eating Out
- ☐ Shopping
- ☐ Traveling
- ☐ Entertainment
- ☐ Other: _____

Describe where you grew up and the impact it has on where you are now.

_____

_____

_____

_____

_____

_____

_____

Time is of the essence. It is the only thing you can not get back. Therefore, this next section is critical. You will set deadlines for goals and recall how you spent time in the past. You will make the decision that this is important and no more time can be wasted.

When

When are you trying to reach your goals?
Give specific time frame/ date for each.

When are you going to pull the trigger and get
started? Be specific.

When

When is the last time you used a budget and stuck to it for more than 6 months? What did you like about? What did you dislike?

_____

_____

_____

_____

_____

_____

When this gets hard, what will be your motivation?

_____

_____

_____

_____

_____

_____

This next section is my personal favorite, by far. Find out your why. You will dig deep and get in tune with why it is even worth making sacrifices to change your situation. Your why is the glue that will hold this process together.

Why

What is your why? Why are you moving forward in this journey to get your money right?

_____

_____

_____

_____

_____

_____

_____

Why does any of this matter to you?

_____

_____

_____

_____

_____

_____

Why

Why have you delayed so long to get started?

Summarize your why in five words or less.

Finally, how are you going to get this done? What is your plan? How is your life going to change? All of these are questions that you will work to answer. There is no doubt that some sacrifices have to be made. Think through foreseeable shifts.

How

How does what you do now impact your future?
your family's future?

How are you going to get it done? Will a plan be
involved?

MIND OVER MONEY

ITS LEVELS TO THIS

How will your lifestyle be impacted as you make changes to reach your goals?

_____

_____

_____

_____

_____

_____

_____

_____

_____

On a scale of 1-10, how bad do you want it? (1 being not bad at all and 10 being so bad I can taste it) _____

MIND OVER MONEY

ITS LEVELS TO THIS

Now that the foundation has been laid and you have an understanding of who you are in regard to your finances and examined your why, it is time to put that heart work into action.

The next step is to track your spending for a month. When I say track it, I mean down to the penny. You need to know exactly where your money is going. You probably think you know where it's going. You might have a general idea. I'm willing to bet that if you've never tracked your money before, there are some things that slip your memory. To get started with this, there are tons of resources you can use. Utilize all the technology around you!

Personally, I like mobile apps that connects directly to my account. Don't like apps? An excel spreadsheet will do the trick. Or use your bank statement, pencil and paper and write it all down.

Sound tedious? The first time you do this will be time consuming. It's like the first time you tied your shoes on your own. It was a little frustrating because you were new to it. But now that you have some practice with it, you can tie your shoes in seconds with minimal effort.

Think of tracking your spending like that. You'll get much better at it as time passes. You might find you have more money that you thought. Or you may find that you are over extending yourself based on your income. Either way knowing the truth about your money will give you powerful information to take control.

What you do with that power is up to you. I would suggest creating a budget that helps you crush the goals you outlined earlier in this workbook.

MIND OVER MONEY

Its Levels to This

It's Levels to This

Level Zero: Laying the Foundation
Level One: Budget Reset
Level Two: Micro Emergency Fund
Level Three: Snowball to Avalanche
Level Four: Mega Emergency Fund
Level Five: Give it Fifteen Percent
Level Six: Debt that Wouldn't Die
Level Seven: Retire Sooner
Level Eight: Mortgage Attack
Level Nine: Live on Fifty Percent
Level Ten: Legacy

Mind Over Money, LLC is a company working to close the wealth gap by promoting financial literacy for individuals, families and communities. This workbook is part of a series that will guide participants to a lifestyle that supports wealth generation and accumulation.

See more from Mind Over Money by visiting the website www.mindovermoney.net

M MIND OVER MONEY